MANIPULATED

*by love, sex,
and depression.*

JESSICA M. PAYES

ISBN (paperback):
979-8-9876863-1-7

ISBN (ebook):
979-8-9876863-0-0

Author Photography:
Thirty1Eighty8

Book Design:
Our Galaxy Publishing

MA·NIP·U·LA·TION:

The action of manipulating someone in a clever
or unscrupulous way.

Sometimes situations arise that are out of our control. We reach for the hands of others and trust that they can guide us, help us, and heal us. Truth is, sometimes these people hurt us more than we ever expected. Sometimes the people we encounter in life are nothing but a lesson. And the lesson in this all is to be self-aware. Understand your fears, your triggers, your emotions both good and bad and spend time with yourself. Fall in love with yourself the way you desperately want others to. The only mistake you make in life is giving someone else power over you. You are stronger than your pain...

I am stronger than my pain.

MANIPULATED

love. — 1

sex. — 23

depression. — 41

*TRIGGER WARNING

love.

"Daddy's Girl."

The first man in my life seemed to be nonexistent
Physically he was there but emotionally he was distant
So, every night I stayed awake praying to God wishing
That one day we could have a bond like the one that we were missing
It was easy to fall behind, always being in the middle
"Pain heals within time" and yet I still remain crippled
Long nights where I called for him, and he was nowhere to be found
Walking in and out emotionally, like a door spinning round
He worked hard, and sacrificed so much for me
I would've known him all my life, but that choice wasn't up to me
See, 'cause, he worked late most days, and days off he spent worn out
His silence broke my brick walled heart, I let him break me down
I wrote a poem about him when I was just about 12 years old
I knew I had a gift in me, just never thought I'd be so bold
The prompt said to write "where you're from, or wish to be"
So, I wrote "I'm from a place where you never seem to be"
In and out of therapy, for over 10 years straight
But you never believed in my disease you said it was always fake
I couldn't trust a professional, because I couldn't have trusted you
It's worse now 'cause I don't know love, 'cause I never had it from you
You find partners like your parents
Pick and choose them then compare them
Then you say he's nothing like your dad, but he's as clear as he's transparent
He's straightforward and he's honest
Says he lies and breaks his promise
But you put him above everyone so he can win your contest
'Cause, love is something strange, it's foreign and it's new
And maybe I'd be less scared of change if you loved me like I loved you
I wanted you to protect me from the scary monsters under my bed
But as I grew older the monsters moved and made their way into my head
I needed you, but you never did come to my rescue
You never wanted to be there for me no matter how much I begged you
You didn't teach me how to love, I had to learn that the hard way
Life's a race here goes the guns and I never got to the start place

You didn't warn me about men, or teach me how to fight
We were under the same roof, but we lived a separate life
You were strict, and you were stern
'To live is the best way learned'
You taught me if I play with fire, I will end up burned

You didn't tell me why or how that fire was always steaming
You taught me the right answers, yeah, but not the correct meanings
So, I walk through life, questioning everyone else's intentions
I mirror back what I get but all I see is your reflection
And, I'm broken
....
Who knows, maybe it's 'cause you are too
Still coping from the fact that your father left you
But because you didn't leave physically
You think it's not killing me
That you and I can't be in the same room for too long acting civilly
Do you even know why I'm always hurting?
Why I spend every weekend working?
It's 'cause I can't stand the thought of us talking face-to-face in person
'Cause, your idea of bonding is you on the couch downing bottles
Then you question why I'm so fucked up as if you were the perfect model
You criticize and you judge, you can't accept me for who I love
You always have the final say and what's been said is what's been done
And, I don't know how much longer I can sit back and remain silent
I always think about telling you how I feel but it's never the right time and
I lose my train of thought and all the words I glued together
'Cause when you look me in the eyes, I choke under all the pressure
And it's the same shit I go through with every single one of my partners
Guns blazing, hearts breaking 'cause I'm fighting without armor
It's that thick skin, that I have
Hurt people hurt people back
**And I never knew how important it is for a daughter to be loved by
her dad**

Daddy issues...
Who would've thought it?
You had love for me before I just wonder when you lost it
Lost it,
All the respect for myself I lost it
There's a thin line between my heart and legs and every boy I meet they
cross it

And I blame you
Because everywhere I turn, I search for acceptance
I search for trust, honesty, and dependence

I keep making mistakes and I never learn my lesson
So, when someone good comes around, I just keep on second guessing
'Cause, the only love I've known was the love I had to fight for
The kind of love you cried out in your bed and stayed up all
night for
The kind of love that hurts if you let it get too close
The kind of love where ignoring meant, "I love you, the most"
And boy, did they love me...
At least, that's what I imagined
How else do you justify their negative words and actions?
My father, my partners, it's all a sick twisted cycle
Of does he love me, does he not, and I can't seem to shake this denial
I wish that you loved me, and I wish that you knew me
Not because I want a bond like the one they show in movies
Not because my outside doesn't match my inner beauty
Not because you feel like using the word "love" really loosely
Not because as a father it's your responsibility and duty
Not because if I die, you're afraid things will get spooky and your lack of
love will always haunt you
I want you to love me for me, but more importantly because you want to.

"I'm Okay."

You left me, and that's okay
Because the memories will forever stay
You hurt me, and that's okay
Because your happiness means more to me than mine does anyway
You met someone, and that's okay
You love her now, and that's okay
You're smiling so much brighter every single day
You shine so bright even through the hardest of rain
And so long as you're happy I could care less about my pain
When you really love someone, I guess that's the price you gotta pay
And you know what? That's okay
Because the tears will stop falling one day
And even if they don't, I'll still be okay
It's all okay because I trusted you
I fell in love with you
You were the one person I admired, I looked up to you
But you led me to believe
That it was only me
Then strung her along the same time you were fucking me
You lied, you cheated
You made promises to me that you could never keep
You ripped
You shattered
You *destroyed* every part of me
Every part I had left, I gave you so effortlessly

I didn't want to trust you
And I didn't want to love you
If I knew right now that it wouldn't be enough for you

You broke everything, all that's left is the pain
All the pieces of me gone
And that's **not** okay.

"9-1-1."

"9-1-1, what's your emergency?"
It started off calm
Like nothing could go wrong
But like all relationships that 'honeymoon phase' don't last long
He bought my love through jewelry and flowers
And there wasn't a love story that compared to ours
He put me on a pedestal, and treated me like royalty
Never did I have to question his morale or loyalty
He held me down, when I needed it most
And I know nobody's perfect, but I swear he came so close
He extended his arms wide whenever I needed his guidance
And always knew what to say even if the answer was silence
It was perfect for months, so I never did expect it
To all go down south and things to get so hectic
It was your typical fights at first
He **yelled, I cried, and things magically seemed to work**
Then somewhere along the lines I started my heavy drinking
And acted out on feelings when I wasn't clearly thinking
It was your typical fights at first
I yelled, *he* **cried, and things magically seemed to work**
Then somewhere along the lines, yelling just wasn't doing it
But I swore I loved him I just had a hard time proving it
I kept apologizing after every hurtful slur
But my apologies meant nothing when the whole night was a blur
Apologizing for events I don't recall occurred
It's absurd,
Looking back on my behavior
Screaming so loud that it woke up the neighbors
Accusing him of cheating with no trail on paper
I put my fist, to his deep dimpled cheeks
And the swelling didn't go down until a couple of weeks
He forgave me, and then the cycle repeats
It was your typical fights at first
I *hit,* **he forgave, and things magically seemed to work**
But somewhere along the lines, these fights grew more intense
Had to *beg* for his forgiveness 'cause this wasn't the first offense
So, earlier today I went out with some of my friends
And started drinking as if the day had no end
But something told me to rush back to his home
Because in the back of my mind, I swore he wasn't alone

I WAS BANGING ON THE DOOR, LIKE I WAS THE POLICE
AND EVERY SECOND THAT WENT BY MY ANGER INCREASED
THERE WAS NO NEED FOR EXPLAINING
'CAUSE I WAS WAY PAST COMMUNICATING
MY ANGER KEPT ESCALATING
AND HE HIT ME...

No hesitation

I fell to the ground, onto a chair, fan, and some cables
And maybe I wouldn't have fallen if I wasn't so unstable
I remember laying on the ground, shocked in disbelief
But, it's okay, because I hit him, so he hit me
But I knew I wasn't safe and that I had to leave
Because there was no stopping him, no matter how much I begged him to please
As I rushed to his room to grab my belongings
He put his hand over my mouth to prevent me from calling
I'm screaming like it's not 4 o'clock in the morning
I just wanted to go home, but I knew I wasn't sober
So, he grabbed my keys until my drunken rant was over
I started to walk out, and he followed close behind
I said "I had to go" and he hit me and said **"FINE!"**

And it's crazy...cause when you're drunk, there's some things you can't recall
But thank God for the blood that was smeared on the walls
I ran outside, hoping anyone could hear me
I waved down to the police but they didn't see me
And the neighbors, get this, wouldn't let *him* anywhere near me
But if only they knew the truth then they too, would fear me
I saw blood gush from my hand, down my leg and onto the street
How could I let this cycle repeat?
And the very next day, I spent in the hospital getting x-rays
Answering the questions they had on the survey
Because I had bruises on *my* wrists,
Bruises on *my* lips
Bruises on *my* arms, back, chest, knees, and hips
It started off calm
How did this go wrong?

Were the signs clearly there and we ignored them all along?
It was your typical fights at first
But after that night, nothing's ever seemed to work
I guess somewhere along the lines he realized this was too intense
I guess somewhere along the lines he found his inner strength
But I don't blame him, because it was self-defense
Because if the roles were reversed, well then, that would make sense.

"My Thorne."

Your smile seems bright
As your eyes fill with light
In a different way from when *I* was still in your life
Your presence is glowing
And your happiness is showing
Its way throughout your body and you don't even know it
Your mood has changed
The way you talk ain't the same
I guess walking out your life is the reason to blame
I guess walking out your life was a blessing to you
Because ever since I left, nothing is upsetting you
So, I don't know why I'm here confessing to you...
There's no doubt in my heart
The feelings I felt were strong from the start
And have only gotten stronger with this time apart
I miss you, I do
But we're opposites, me and you
It was a really great thing at first then it turned bad too
Many fights with our fists and guns blazing
After the nights that were so amazing
But neither of us knew what we were truly facing
A lifetime of hate, jealousy, and rage
Trapped with each other like an animal in a cage
How can we be together when we're not on the same page?
I want your happiness to outshine the sun
But I have failed you all these years, so I think my time is done
We're better off parting ways in the long run

All I ever wanted was someone like you...
Not *someone* like you,
All I ever wanted was you

Yet, I failed and failed you too many times before
So, this cuts me deep, deep down to the core
When I say I can't be with you anymore
I didn't want to speak those words into existence
Because I never thought breaking up would've existed
And now all you are to me is a memory in the distance
And every day I wake up praying and wishing
That we can just live in the moment so I can stop reminiscing

I miss it...
The late-night calls and random texts
The fights, your hugs, and makeup sex
The "I love you's" were always the best
Memories like yours I will never forget
But your heart was too strong, and I was too weak
I made promises to you I knew I couldn't keep
So now I sit back and wallow in my own grief
Thinking about all the goals we set to achieve
Are now the ones that are incomplete
Your love was different, than the others
The kind of love you hope to discover
That makes the dead of winter feel like the beginning of summer
The kind of love that makes you think "is this even real?"
The type of emotions you never thought you'd feel
From wounds and scars you ***never*** thought would heal
But everything does, and it feels so right
The happiest you've been so far in your life
Makes every battle worth every fight
But, with fighting comes tears
And all of my fears
That we won't make it in the next couple of years
So, how do we part, and say goodbye nicely
When the words I'm saying aren't being put lightly
The chances of us fixing things is highly unlikely
I'm sorry things just can't seem to work
And just so you know, I never intended to make you hurt
Or to disrespect you and your self-worth,
But I did,
And no amount of apologies could take that all back
All the selfish things I've done to you in the past
Or all the things I should've done but I always lacked
You deserve someone who can cherish you
Someone you can see a future with and might get married to
Not someone who will let you jump straight into love without a parachute
I am not her; I will never be who you need
This is the best thing for us, even if we don't agree
So, goodbye my love, move on and be free
You will always be my favorite memory.

"Closure."

I called you last night, and I wish I had a better reason
But it's time I stop running and time I start feeling
I'm confused,
It's been days, months, and years since I've felt pain from you
Since I've felt pain, at all
See 'cause, it was right after you, that I needed alcohol
And I don't blame you for my addiction
But ever since you left, nothing's ever been more different
And by different, I mean shattered
The pain you rooted in me caused nothing else to matter
When you told me it was over
It was the last day I was sober
It was the last day I was faithful
And I've never gotten closure
'Cause you chose her
After you told me you wouldn't
So, I carry my bags and unload them even when I know that I shouldn't
But you did that
The trust issues I have, you built that
And it only took you 8 weeks
It's been 4 years now and I still haven't made peace
'Cause looking back at it, when I was with you, I wasn't drinking
My mind was shut off and my heart did all the thinking
And it played me,
Alcohol isn't ruining my life, it is trying to save me
From the pain you inflicted
I thought I knew who you were, I thought you were different
I trusted you,
And to me that means more than saying "I love you"
'Cause the doors I spent closing for my heart's preservation
I opened them to you without hesitation
And I didn't mean to trust you, it happened so suddenly
And I didn't mean to love you, it happened so subtly
You made me feel every emotion
Maybe that's why now I feel so very broken
I felt envy, I felt rage
I felt happy and afraid
I felt sad the day you left me,
All alone, I felt betrayed
And now,

I feel nothing unless I pour these shots down
I felt nothing the day you stopped coming around
I feel...
N o t h i n g
Because you hurt me so bad
And I refuse to feel again if it's anything like that
Do you know, you were the last person I was good to?
What did I do to deserve this, how could you?
You lied when I demanded your honesty
You made me feel like there was something wrong with me
You had me so conditioned
So now I ignore my intuition
And I say "you're all the same" 'cause I can't tell no more who's different
Because you were supposed to be
You made me feel loved, your arms were home to me
And now, I'm homeless
I search for love in the streets but I see now it's hopeless
'Cause I will never again allow myself that uncertainty
Of someone saying they love me, then just end up hurting me.

"Her First Love."

It was puppy love
At least that's what they called it
"As quickly as it came it's gone,"
But we never did fall for it
We fell for each other, both so deep and wrapped tightly
And if this isn't love, then I'm scared of what it might be
Because I've seen so many people walk in, and then leave
So many hearts shattered and left at the scene
And I know you're afraid he'll break my heart at eighteen
But Mom, please let me marry the man of my dreams
I love him, I swear, I put that on God
And I know you can't resist the man you look up to a lot
He's in my prayers, Mom
I pray that he's strong
I pray for our love and hope nothing goes wrong
I pray for our future, I want a home and six kids
And I've never wanted anything more than I've ever wanted this
Mama, please say you'll say yes
Whether you think you know what's best
Put your fear aside and help me pick out my white dress
Because I am marrying that man, whether or not you are a guest
...
I remember our first kiss, skipping class holding hands
We even played together in our school's marching band
We talked all hours of every waking day
Our love was so strong, God himself, couldn't take it away
Communication is key, and we were like janitors
But still they told us our love was too young and amateur
Don't tell me we're too young, that we're dumb and naïve
'Cause I heard my own father scream love then pack his bags up and leave
I've seen marriages fail, I am aware of the statistics
But our love has jumped through hoops and proven its persistence
...
And just as he was ready to give up all the stress
I said "Babe! Guess what...she said yes!"
Shopping frantically for flowers, shoes, and a veil
It's a dream come true, my own personal fairytale
I shed tears of excitement, shed tears of relief
I finally get to marry the man of my dreams.

"I Do."

Wedding bells ringing
Church choir singing
As we step out as "Mr. and Mrs."
Showing our affection with hugs and kisses
My mom shed tears, as she saw me in white
Seeing me the happiest I've been so far in my life
Freshly nineteen, with my heart filled to the rim
So thankful to have met someone like him
Someone who will love me without hesitation
Without any limits, without expiration
We vowed forever, for richer or poor
And to start a family with him, was all I was hoping for
We were young in love, and infatuated
Drunk off love, completely intoxicated
He was my drug, and I was severely addicted
'Cause a life without him was a life I couldn't live in…
Unfortunately, our love story had to be rewritten
Because the ending was something no one could've predicted
He was dying, and I had not the slightest clue
That our only memory as husband and wife was when we said, "I do."

"My Guardian Angel."

They say with time, pain eases
That your heart will learn to love again even in tiny pieces
That no matter how badly this affects you right now
You'll fight this feeling someway, somehow
The cut is still fresh, as you were just put to rest
But the memories they live, I will never forget
The excitement in your eyes as I walked through the door
I didn't know then, what you were so happy for
But ever since you left, no one could ever love me more
On the days I was sick, you were right by my side
You'd run so fast when you heard me cry
But where are you now?
As I drown myself in tears saying goodbye
Goodbye? Did I really just say those words?
To someone I love, nothing can be worse
Than losing the person who meant the universe
You'll never know
How hard it was to let you go
How much it sucked to hear the news
To know there was nothing I can do
Because in a split second, I already lost you
And now I'm lost too
Because now, my days are dreadful long and empty
It's only been a couple, but it feels like a century
I stay up late at night tossing and turning
'Cause I can't stop thinking and my heart won't stop yearning
For the day you burst in and say you're returning
I wasn't ready…you left without warning
You left me without practice on how to mourn and
Now I struggle to lift my head high
Because no amount of "it'll be okays" will ever apply
To the amount of pain I feel inside
Crying…and it won't seem to end
Why did I have to lose my best friend…
I see you in my dreams,
And you smiled as I touched your face
Then you tell me what it's like to be in a "better place"
Because that's what they say right?
"A better place"
But tell me, how can it be better when between us is so much space

When the only thing I want to feel is your embrace
But from here to heaven there's no staircase
I remember seeing your eyes light up, right before you left me
Then, I remember seeing your eyes dazed out, blank, and empty
Your body was still, but your heart was so strong
The last breath you took was wrapped in my arms
I just wish there was another way you could live on…
When I saw your grave dug, six feet deep
I-
…
I-I nearly choked on my tears and dropped to my feet
Because that's the last sight I wanted to see

…
I couldn't watch when they started to bury him
Because they accidentally threw rocks and I screamed "YOU'RE HURTING HIM!!"
But he wasn't getting hurt, because nothing can hurt him anymore
So, I don't know what I was so upset for
It'll never be the same without him by my side
The hardest thing I had to do was say goodbye
Because I,
Saw his heartbeat go one…two…three…four
One…two…no, more…
In the blink of an eye, and with the touch of a button
He was gone, and I was left with nothing.

Dear Mom,

I wonder how long it'd take you to realize this poem is about you
Would you understand the theme?
Or would the truth make you so uncomfortable you'll pretend to act like
you have no idea what I mean?
Are you even listening?
Because there is so much I have to say
Anger and resentment I can no longer contain
They say to get over your fears you must first confront your pain
So,
Let's chat
I'm pretty blunt with how I feel and I don't think you ever liked that
So, I never invited you to my shows
Not that you ever really asked to go
You just always assumed the answer would be no
When in actuality, I would've loved to have seen you and my dad sitting
front row
Screaming "run that shit back"

But because you're uncomfortable with being uncomfortable I've had to
let go of the idea I could ever experience that

THIS IS BIGGER THAN POETRY

I just wrote to cope

Almost drowned in my emotions and you never sent a boat
House full of fucking family but I always felt alone
Have you even read the book that I just fucking wrote?

I don't
Mean to sound harsh
But this is who I am
I talk about my feelings, and I win poetry slams

I'm a fucking published author
And I never wanted to go to school
I only went to make you happy, and I still never got that approval

It's cool tho,
Couple years of therapy, and I'm straight chillin'

Writing down my thoughts cause I'm not good with my feelings
Wanna have a talk like adults since I've been real into healing
But I'm afraid you won't understand and we'll end up disagreeing
Like
We did just today at 1 o'clock
I had someone tell me "you can't listen if you're speaking" and the problem
is, you never stop

So, I learned to be silent
Learned how to twist my emotions private
From the people I love the most

Strangers know me better than you ever will because they know what I've
been through and you don't

And it sucks
Maybe it's bad luck

I'm not saying you didn't love me,
I'm saying **I didn't feel loved enough**

And maybe that was my perception
Seeing life through my depression
Always questioned if it's real not how I feel and assumed it was for
attention

And even if it was
I still ain't fucking get it

Focusing on what causes less stress because you already got three
headaches
And I didn't want to bother you

So here I am
With a mic in my hand
Hoping you'll understand that sometimes my depression doesn't go
according to your life's plans
Or mine
Because in case you forgot it's been only two years since I attempted
suicide
And I still cry about it

Wondering why you ain't jump off that plane
I know I'm not the type to ask for help but as a mother, you should've

known your daughter was in so much pain

But you barely batted a lash
Went away for the weekend, knocked on my door like
"Hey I'm back, still sad? Great chat."

And I know you gon' say I exaggerated that,
Like it ain't happen like that
Like all the tears I cry are lies and I imagine all that

I just want to be heard
Without yelling, interrupting, or twisting my words
I want you to acknowledge that it hurts
'Cause,
All my life I've been looked at as the issue, when the truth is, you never
bothered to look in the mirror first.

sex.

"Inside."

As a woman, your worth is determined by who's in your bed
And your value decreases the more times you open your legs
And like a 7-11, not a day goes by closed
'Cause they never taught you self-respect it was never shown
So the "know your worth" never works
Like the "love yourself" and "put you first," it's all words
Of a language you can't seem to grasp
'Cause you don't know what it means to take things slow you always moved way too fast
And, you're out of breath
They say a piece of you goes missing every time that you have sex
And you gave out so many pieces that you don't have any left
And now, all you feel is hollow
'Cause they lead you to the bedroom and all you do is follow
Left, right, left, right and sometimes you wish you've forgotten how to walk
They say a woman's body is an elaborate map and sometimes you wish they got lost
In your eyes, not in your thighs
Physical attraction is common in most, but beauty comes from who is inside

So, who's inside?

"Scarlet Letter."

I'm laying down on your side of my bed
Wishing the pillows I cry into were your arms instead
I'm reaching out, eyes shut, with my lips quivering
As I try to hold onto your smell that's still lingering
It smells like arrogance, betrayal, and mostly dishonesty
Like the acceptance of a hurt that never got an apology
You are nonexistent,
Physically you are there, but emotionally you are distant
It sounds too familiar,
Like I've said these words aloud
I can scream DADDY ISSUES all I want, but I am talking to a deaf crowd
Because they listen 'til I'm ready to slip down my pants
'Til I'm vulnerable enough to give them a chance
I fall right into their traps, and play right into their hands
"WYD"
A three-letter text that's got me eager to leave
Eager and willing to spend a night or three
With men I do not know and are not right for me
"YO"
Another text I get sent at night
Followed by "YOU UP?" at 3am or those big emoji eyes
"WASSUP?"
And sometimes I think that I'm asking for too much
But I'm not looking to date I'm just looking to fuck
But I'm not looking for lust, I'm looking for love
Honestly, I can't even tell the difference
I let men like you in, without the fear of commitment
With every ounce of liquor, I find myself drinking
It's easy to mask the pain than ever really admitting,
I'm scared…
What if I find love and I'm not prepared?
Or worse, what if I get hurt? More than I've already been
See, love is too strong of a game and I never seem to win
'Cause after the hangover fades, and I've caught another body
I can never rid the shame that's permanently tattooed on me
Like the Scarlet Letter, everyone sees me and can see that I'm damaged
And nobody wants somebody when everybody's already had it
So, they never call me after sex
And after the third unanswered text,
I get drunk again and I'm onto the next

See after Bryan, there was Reese, Tyrone, Mitch and James
So many guys in my bed, and I don't even know all their names
And I try to flip the script, but the story still remains
They get all the sex, and I get all the pain.

"Guys Like You."

I can't tell if it's guys like you, or girls like me
Who reflect and project their insecurities
Who neglect and accept all the immaturity
To perfect and protect a man you know he could never be
A woman, I can never be
See,
I think it's time that I start to accept
That I'm always the girl you call just to have sex
I'm the girl who never wins, I'm not even second best
I'm the girl who always stays, but always gets left
I am naïve,
I give more love to others than I have ever received
I'm so desperate for compassion because somewhere I believe
That falling in love is a goal I can achieve
But, I guess I gotta accept the fact that, that'll never be me.

"Master of Manipulation."

"Don't piss me off"
I'm sorry, was it something I said
"Don't piss me off you're doing it again"
I'm sorry, getting you mad was never part of my intentions
I didn't even say anything, I ain't even mention the—
You know what, never mind, because you'll always end up right
And I'm not in the mood to lose another fight
'Cause you'll raise your voice, and I'll cower in fear
Trying to dodge the disrespect and cover my tears
'Cause, I can't show you I'm weak, because you love the control
I'm a prisoner for your love and you'll never grant me parole
You feed me words that are backhanded compliments
Like "look who's finally listening and learned some common sense
What do you bring to the table besides your pussy and ass?
You know, I don't like that many people but you're not all that bad"
Hands on my lap, mouth shut, and I'm frozen too
If there's one thing you taught me was to speak when you are spoken to
Yes sir
No sir
Please, and *always* thankful
Incur
Recur
And each time it's more painful
But my feelings stick out, like a big sore thumb
I don't think I'm building a tolerance I think I'm getting more dumb
'Cause I've read books about guys like you
About the different stages and phases of abuse
About the cycle that never ends
And the women who sweep it under the rug and just play pretend
And I was always so angry at the women who remained stagnant
In relationships filled with self-hatred and sadness
And they stay...
I, stay...
And I can't quite put my finger on it, the reason I keep coming
I guess it's better to be treated like shit than to be treated like nothing
I'd rather settle for the yelling, the screaming, the roaring disrespect
The low-quality dead-end meaningless sex
I'd trade it all for healthy but that just makes too much sense
I like the complications
The fights and intimidation

Why else would leaving cause such a hesitation
I need your approval, even if I only get it once weekly
I just have to know that in a world so ugly, there's someone out there that needs me
Because when the dust begins to settle, and the flames die down
You know, you're actually not that bad to be around
But when the fires lit, oh God, it combusts
And I take a step back and I look back at us
And **I AM NOT HAPPY...**
I'm not happy...
But I will deny it to my grave if anyone ever asks me
Because I love the complications
The fights and intimidation
But there's nothing I love more than the master of manipulation
And that's you.

"Stay Blessed, Beloved."

NO
It's my turn to speak,
I let you overpower me now it's your turn to feel weak
It's your turn to shut up, cause I'm tired of being silent
Used to cower away in fear but I am thru with all the hiding
I should've slapped you with respect the first time I heard your voice raise
But fucked boys will be fuckboys in their own fucked up boy ways
Yo,
Truthfully,
I've never met someone more fucked up than you
You probably think it's a compliment
But I don't expect you to understand cause you confuse narcissism with confidence
Lack of power with dominance
Inability with competence
Just because you're not where you want to be in life doesn't mean you have the right to downplay my accomplishments
Who the fuck do you think you are?
Cause last time I checked you only made me come, to my senses
I realized it wasn't the type of men I chose, it was the kind of love I accepted
And I accepted you
So I protected you

On days your voice echoed hate in my soul I still respected you...

But, you never did deserve my kindness
Cause there's no getting thru to someone so empty minded
Someone so weak and spineless
Someone stubborn and defiant
It's amazing how a man could act so fucking childish

But I can't change you
Shit, I can't even fucking blame you
Life's let you down too many times I know that must be painful

But,
It's important knowing when to give up
So ladies take this with you any time that you feel stuck
Refer his ass to therapy and wish him the best of luck
Because as long as he is damaged you will never be enough

"Fuck Him."

He said he needed time, then outta nowhere he just dipped
No two weeks or nothing, and he ain't even tell you shit
Caught off guard, 'cause you thought things were alright
Now you crying staring at his IG all night
'Cause you catching the subs and passive aggressive posting
Said he likes to keep a private life but he's out here boasting
'Bout his next big moves, 'bout his next big shots
'Bout how he's so proud to be fucking with these thots
He's deliberate
Inconsiderate
You gave him your heart and words can't describe what he did to it
But, all that bad shit fades
And all that pain goes away
When you hear his fucking voice, or see his stupid face
He's got you hypnotized, like you're in some kind of trance
So he manipulates you into thinking that he's worth another chance
But there comes a point in time when you realize what you're worth
So, you leave and don't look back no matter how much it hurts
'Cause it kills you
To know the person who empties your heart was the same who used to fill you
But you keep your "head straight" and take his advice

So, you crying at home but post "I'm living my best life"
Then you see his followers skyrocket and
You finally build the courage to unfollow and block him
Then shorty posts some pics, and he dies of dehydration
But remember y'all broke up, so he owes no explanation
He left you, 'cause he wasn't ready to take the next step
Then you catch his ass on tinder and he ain't swiping to the left
He's got a new girl, he's talking oh so slick too
Thinks he's in love 'cause she puts up with his shit and gave it up quick too
Now she's getting the same treatment you had
Getting fill ins to match his fucking durag
You mad
Mad he wasn't man enough to wanna build and stay
Mad he's giving her the love he should've gave you from the first day
It hurts, don't it?
To be left out of the team and treated like an opponent
To know yesterday he said your name, but now it's her name that he's

moaning
It's her name on his phone, and it's her name he stays calling
And it's her bed now he's waking up to every morning
When it should've been you
'Cause it could've been you
You tried everything on Earth so that it would've been you
But would've, could've, should've, doesn't stitch up your cuts
And would've, could've, should've, doesn't fix y'all back up
'Cause now she's got his attention
She's riding with him but ain't got no sense of direction
So y'all can have your matching sets
And y'all can have your trashy sex
Just watch out for him sis, 'cause he'll do you dirty next
'Cause he's a **FUCKBOY**
He walks, talks and traps like one
Claiming he's a real man but never acts like one
And you feel stupid for believing him
Stupid for seeing something he don't even see in him
He used to laugh at you, but guess who's laughing still
It's true, 'when a good woman leaves your life everything goes downhill'
'Cause he got, NO JOB, and NO AMBITION
NO GOALS, JUST HOPEFUL WISHING
And now he wanna text you like everything's just fine
It's like he got an alert on his phone that he finally left your mind
Now you're feeling so torn, like Letoya Luckett
Part of you wants to respond but the other half says fuck it
So you're burning a hole thru your screen just staring at his name
Thinking "how can he be so nonchalant after causing so much pain"
After not giving a fuck,
About leaving so abrupt
He **DOES NOT** have the right to come back once you finally gave up
Once you crossed him out your heart, once you crossed him out your mind
That shit was not easy it took a long time
For you to feel okay, and not that "fake it 'til you make it"
You can bounce back from a scratch, but he took your heart to break it
He took all of your feelings and tried to manipulate it
HE FUCKED YOU RAW SO MANY TIMES THEN CLAIMED Y'ALL NEVER DATED
FUCK HIM.

"Fuck You."

You must think you so slick huh?
Acting like a bitch still stressing you
Yeah I know it was Christmas the day I hit you, but that ain't why I messaged you
You ain't been a thought in my mind for a minute
Shit,
Damn near forgot you existed
Came so close to pushing my limits but boy, I worked hard for this mindset and spirit
You can't kill this
Not no more
See, your time has come to an end
And I promise so long as I'm writing I'm not waisting another rhyme on you again
Because you WILL NOT destroy my peace, my patience, or my poems especially
'Cause it's always gonna be fuck boys, "fuck him" and FUCK YOU... respectfully.

"After Hours."

You crave me only when light fades to darkness
A crave for love but a love so heartless
With a single text, young and naïve
I'm on the road doing full speed
Racing to your house like the **IDIOT** that I am
Pretending that I could be alright
Going to your house in the middle of the night
When being with you makes the tears harder to fight
But when you ask me "What's wrong?"
I say "I'm just fine."
As if you really care what's on my mind
Quit talking to me, you're just wasting our time
I'm here for business only, aren't I?
This is what I had started originally
Didn't think I'd care at first, but now it's kinda hitting me
Like a shot straight to the chest
And it was clear from the beginning this was all about sex
And believe me it was but now I'm trying my best
Trying my best to keep my mouth shut
It's okay to have sex with me every night casually but to be something more I'm not good enough
You can commit to having casual sex
But too afraid to commit and take the next step
Like a cordless phone, no emotional attachments
You and I used to mean something, what the fuck happened?
So, tell me
Why can you get off in treating me the way that you do
And even when I know I deserve someone better I *still* come running back to you
Time and time again, after I just finished hurting
And what kills me the most is you don't have the decency to treat me like a person
After what we just did?
And I can't get a goodnight kiss?
Is there something wrong with my lips?
Because you didn't seem to have a problem when they were all over your dick
And now you throwing me out your house as if I never meant shit
As if you never wanted this
As if I made the whole thing up in my head and this never did exist

BUT NO

But no...
This is what I signed up for, and this is what we agreed to
Too weak to go on without you but I hate admitting that I need you
So, I settled for the casual things and whatever I could to please you
'Cause seeing you every now and then
Was better than never seeing you again
But look at me here, stuck at a dead end
Praying and hoping we could be something more when I can't even call you my friend
I loved you
And you used me
And I just let you
So how can I move on freely when you made it so hard to forget you
And you can't see
How hard it is for me
To go to your house and have sex casually
Knowing that this is all it'll ever be
Knowing that is my worth to you
Knowing that this isn't affecting or hurting you like the way it's killing me
I was stupid to think that "after hours" could ever more to you
But I'm smart enough now to know I'm nothing but a whore to you
But stupid enough still, to open all the doors for you
But now I'm racing off, in the opposite direction
Avoiding confrontation and avoiding rejection
But you run to me and follow me and force to say what's wrong with me
and the conversation goes as follows:
"It's best if I don't say it, you don't wanna hear it anyways
You never cared about me before what makes tonight different than the other days"
"You seem stressed just tell me please what's on your mind"
"For the millionth time, I swear to god I'm just fine!!"
Running away again, banging my hands into the steering wheel
That was my golden opportunity to tell you how I feel
Crying all through the night
Crying when I hit the red light
I pick up my phone and I start texting your name
Thinking to myself "you're not worth all this pain"
So the text I sent was something I thought you should know
"I just can't keep doing this anymore" and your response was:
"So don't"
And by that time, it was clear to me
That sex was all this appeared to be
But I just couldn't get up and leave

Because I wanted every part of you
So making the decision to leave was the hardest I had to do
Knowing my worth, and saying it to myself constantly
Another lesson learned, but everyday still haunting me
And I will **NEVER** be that girl you call to have sex with and then just dismiss
It took me way too long to realize, but I know now that I am so much better than this shit.

"Blackout."

You said you didn't mean to...
And that you were caught in a moment
But when I say the word "RAPE," you never seem to own it
I should've known better, because this has happened way before
And every time I think I'm loved I give it my all and more
So, maybe I'm to blame for this, because I read all the warnings
And this isn't the first time I woke up to someone in the morning
I-I know it looks bad...but I swear I didn't want to
Because a decision made in the heat of the moment is the one that always haunts you
I left my house that night...without any intention of having sex
But when liquor gets involved there's no telling what happens next
I don't remember what was said...but I know I made the call
But tell me, how can you get consent from someone who's bumping into walls
Someone with slurred speech, closed eyes, and every five seconds that goes by falls
I woke up naked...physically and emotionally
As you smiled at me...cynically and soullessly
Are you proud of yourself?
Do you feel like 'the man?'
Like you accomplished a goal that was part of your life plan?
Do you feel **WHOLE?**
Like the way I feel *e m p t y?*
You could've chose someone else, *anyone* else, I'm sure consenting women there's plenty
I justified your actions 'cause I didn't think I could be raped
And when I think of that word, I think of held against your will, or being duct taped
I KNEW THAT RED MEANT STOP, AND THAT GREEN MEANT GO
BUT I DIDN'T THINK A DRUNK YES MEANT A SOBER NO
I remember throwing up in my bathroom sink
Because I couldn't hold down any more of my drink
I was incoherent, and unable to consent, wouldn't you think?
Shouldn't you have thought twice before helping me get undressed
Before you put your hands through my hair and kissed down from my neck
Before you—
...I can't remember the rest

I was too drunk to slow down the pace we had fastened
And how can I feel pain from a memory pitch black and,
How can I call this rape, when I'm not even sure it happened
I had to ask you why I was laying down unclothed
You spoke nothing but the truth but I wish lies you told
'Cause now this black memory I am forced to hold
BECAUSE EVERY BIT OF INNOCENCE I HAD LEFT YOU STOLE
So, let me ask you something
Did it ever occur to you to stop...just once?
Please answer the question I've been dying to know, for months
I suppressed this horrific blackened memory
That damaged my mind and put my life in jeopardy
I was two weeks late and thought it could be yours
You said you wore a condom but how do I know that for sure?
How do I know that you took all the necessary precautions
When you did this to me when I was unconscious
I was belligerent and a mess
How could you even enjoy the sex
It's not fair that you get to discard this memory and I can *never* forget
You look me in my eyes, and feel no remorse
You said "we're both grown adults" so that gives you the right to force
Your way through a door I didn't unlock for you
But you were determined to get in and there was no stopping you
You stripped me down and now every day I walk alone and naked
And actively try to restore all the damage that you created
But, I gotta give it to you tho, 'cause it takes someone real brave
To have the audacity to not call what you did rape
Now let me ask you something else, 'cause I just can't seem to let it go
Did you rape me drunk because you knew if I was sober, I'd say no?

"White-out."

I finally worked the nerve to read you back my poem
Because it's time that I take back all my innocence you have stolen
I spent years wishing it was all a dream
And I spent tears on lowering my self-esteem
'Cause I fell victim to depression,
Using bodily expression
Tryna drown the pain in bottles cause I'm so good at suppression
You would think it's my profession
You would think I learn my lesson
But in the room of my attacker I am currently undressing
See,
I thought if I took control, I wouldn't be so 'triggered'
But EVERY TIME I close my eyes you are the ONLY ONE I picture
It's like flashbacks
With anxiety attacks
To have sex with someone else and I can NEVER relax
To just break down and cry every time I climax
Staring blankly into space 'cause I am so fucking detached

Thanks for that

No...I mean it,

Thank you
Because
You taught me what it meant to be broken and damaged
And showed me my strength when I thought I couldn't manage
Added fuel to the fire and ignited my passion
Turned my pain into words and my words into talent
Learned forgiveness of others when the sorry is absent
And I never would've learned this if this never would've happened

Thanks for the trauma.

depression.

"First Date Questions."

What if I told you, I wasn't okay?
And the only reason I called was to make the suicidal thoughts go away
What if I said I'm too scared to be alone
And even though it's childish you bring me peace over the phone
What if I sobbed uncontrollably?
Would you hang up immediately or stay on the phone with me
And if I drop the call on purpose, would you keep calling until you get a hold of me
What would you do if I said I couldn't explain how I feel?
Would you tell me it's in my head and that my pain is not real
Or would you hold me when I'm lonely and pray one day my scars will heal
Tell me,
Because this isn't up for debate
My anxiety and my depression will always come on our dates
And I'd rather tell you now before you find out way too late
Before you find me on my bed, just wallowing in my sadness
With the negativity in my head I cling to you just like a magnet
So, with all that being said, is this a life you can imagine
Because you and I, are the kind of opposites that never end up attracting
Is it okay...that I'm not?
I'm just trying to make you comfortable I understand that it's a lot
I understand if you want to bail, you can leave before your entrance
'Cause my mind is like a jail and depression is a life sentence
And there are NO visitors...
Am I making myself clear?
There will be days I want you far but times I need you here
Like when my thoughts take control and I hear these voices in my head
That whisper such sweet nothings like I'm better off just being dead
Cutting deeper in the skin, and closer to the vein
I don't cut because it hurts, I cut to feel the pain
And I don't mean to cut you off, I'm just cutting to the chase
'Cause I like to take things slow, but depression has its own pace
So, these are all the things I struggle with internally
But anyways, my favorite color is burgundy.

"Replaced."

I'm scared...
I'm scared to get too close
I'm scared I'll lose you right when it hurts the most
Right when the weight of the world is sitting on my shoulders
And right when my anxiety is about to topple over
Right when I need you...
It's terrifying to think
As quickly as you entered my life, you're gone in the next blink
The next second, I'm screaming into my trembling palms
Crying...where did this go wrong
I told you I needed your support, and you just laughed in my face
I reached out for your hands and all I got was space
Empty...
When I ask for help and you're not there
Empty...
When I play it off like I don't care
Right when I need you...
But she's all you need
It's okay, I get it, it's a better view from the backseat
I've watched everyone I know walk away with a piece of me
I needed you more than you ever needed me
I need you...
Right now,
Because these nights are dark
Because I'm running out of room on my body to make this bloody art
Because every time something good comes along it always falls apart
And I'm tired of having to glue back these pieces of my heart
I'm sorry I'm flawed, and that you have to reassure me
Every second of everyday because of my high insecurities
But can you blame me?
She's beautiful, outside and in
She's smart, she's funny, she's talented and thin
She's everything I'm not, but she's all I want to be
Because maybe if I'm her, then maybe you'd want me
I'm alone, and I miss the days when you were blind
When I was the only thing that consumed your mind
When I had your devoted undivided attention
When I had your heart without any extension
I need you...
Please tell me you'll be there

Don't tell me you're another thing in my life I have to cut up and share
Because all my life, I've had people take and take and take
And when they look her in her eyes, I get replaced, replaced, replaced
She's my sister,
She's my neighbor,
She's my coworker,
She's my friend,
She's the girl you follow on Instagram, the list just never ends
See, cause, it doesn't matter who she is, it matters who I'm not
And even if I were the last person on Earth, she'd still take my spot.

"Caged Thoughts."

Sometimes, I wish I didn't open my mouth
Sometimes, I wish I didn't open my heart
Sometimes, I wish I didn't open anything
Doors, my ears, my mind
My eyes...
Sometimes I wish I wasn't alive
And by alive I don't mean breathing
When I say "please kill me now" I don't mean in life I mean with these feelings
'Cause depression is insane
Has you seeing the world up in flames
And no amount of antidepressants can help the chemical imbalance in your brain
'Cause it's larger than that
It comes then it goes so it gets harder to track
And when it's here it's bad
I'm talking 'bout withdrawn from all endeavors
With feelings of incompetence that doesn't end ever
That doesn't end well
That doesn't blend well
With the way society thinks I should feel, I'd be damned hell
If they try to cage my feelings like I'm in a damn cell

My mind is an animal, and I am my own prey
And when an animal is hungry nothing can get in its way
And when it's done, depression will still eat at my carcass
Defeated and helpless and into the darkness
I am dead
With a smile on my face that's so hard to pretend
And the weight on my chest it's not hard to resent
The people who carry their lives with content
Is the person I wish I could be once again
Why can't I be like them?
I want to so badly,
I don't want to change who I am
I just want to be happy
I just want to feel alive
I just want to feel inside
I just want to see the world from a different set of eyes
I just want to want to live

I don't want to feel like this
I just want to walk through life one day and know what happy is.

"Evicted."

Do you wanna know what lives rent free in my head?

Depression.

And let me tell you, she is not the bear to poke
She is the comedian of all mental health, and I am at the center of every one of her jokes

And I gotta say it's a real knee slap
The way she lowers my self-esteem like I don't fucking need that

She knows exactly what I don't want
Takes control when things go wrong
She's the understudy of my life and is always ready to go on

And steal
The show
My happiness
And more importantly, my confidence

Cause boy does my depression have a way with her compliments

I mean wow...

She yells my deepest insecurities to my ear through a speaker

And I know I'm not supposed to but some days, I actually believe her

And on those days, I wish she'd pay her fucking rent so I can finally meet her

And tell her she's evicted

And that freeloader anxiety isn't welcomed either.

"Homesick."

Depression has a way of making white sand, and clear water
Feel like,
The day we buried my grandfather
Still...
With my feet in the ocean
I'm just going through the motions
Wondering, if this doesn't make me happy, what ever will?
Am I destined to be depressed?
Because lately, it seems like the only thing I do best
Lately it seems like all I ever am is fucking stressed
And lately it seems like the more I get off, the more pressure falls on my chest
I'm uncomfortable
Uneasy
Awkward
And embarrassed
I wonder if they know I feel this way, and that's why they keep staring
I just want to go home
Where the closets aren't filled with last season's depression
Where the mirror projects a more positive reflection
Where my mind and my body create the strongest connection
And the sight of self-love shines through every dimension
I just want to go home
To a place that is free of all negativity
Where the voices stop screaming but sing proudly in symphonies
Where depression no longer keeps me kept in captivity
I just want to go home, to a person I can love
I just wish I were home...
But I never knew exactly where that was.

"Monkey Bars of Hope."

I've been over-thinking
Been in my head so much lately I started over-drinking
I started over-talking, I started over-sharing
I started over-feeling, but never over-caring
Not about myself
Not about the damper I put on my mental health
Not about my wrists and the scars that I've caused
Not about the victories, but every battle I've ever lost
It always comes back to me
And maybe I'd stand a chance fighting if instead it came back gradually
But no matter what I do, this depression stays attacking me
And I just keep losing,
I put my best foot forward like they tell me so I don't know what more I
should be doing
Should I, surround myself with people when all I'm feeling is alone
Or should I mask the pain in bottles because that's all I've ever known?
Should I talk about it? Because that helps right?
But we all know a person with depression never does and if they do it's a
rare sight
'Cause it's swept under the rug
And no one gives a fuck
Then when you're chained down to a hospital bed, they wanna ask "where
is this coming from?"
Everyone is so fucking oblivious
Depression isn't when they run out of your pumpkin spice latte Becky,
It's serious
It's caused me anxiety, and anxiety caused me nightmares
So, I wrestle my mind to sleep and it never seems to fight fair
Sometimes, I break down…I mean, really break down
My moods used to swing but now depressions my playground
And the inner child in me, is on the *monkey bars of hope*
Hanging so tightly so I don't fall in the **unhealthy ways to cope**
And I always thought if I just stood there, I'd never take the loss
See, depression *is* the monkey bars and I've never made it across.

"3:28am"

The truth about depression is
It's unpredictable
Unwarranted
Unpleasant
Unapologetic
It's made me do and say terrible things to myself without ever asking for
forgiveness because depression makes you feel
Unworthy
Unwanted
Unloved
It's made me believe that I would be better if I just give up
And by give up, I mean suicide
Let's just cut the bullshit
'Cause you can ask all these "prescreening questions" and I promise I am
the full list
"Do you ever have trouble sleeping?
Loss of interest in activities?
Do you struggle getting out of bed just to avoid daily responsibilities?
Do you find yourself feeling empty?
And that your life is losing purpose?"
It's funny they ask these questions when depression has different versions
So, let me tell you how it hits me
Head high walking down the street and it comes out and kicks me
Emotions bleeding out but there's no one here to fix me
Laying helpless on the concrete thinking,
"God, why did they pick me..."

It's cold here...
There's no soul here...
I'm in the deepest cave of my own body and I am alone here...

Everything is black and white
And, it doesn't help when people keep on trying to send me light
'Cause the truth about depression, it knows with who to pick its fights
And I've been beaten up repeatedly
And we all know snitches get stitches so I've dealt with it in secrecy
Learned to let it just eat at me
Learned to let it take its course and hope it leaves peacefully
Only,
It never does

And sometimes I think I'm better off just going nuts
Cause,
The truth about depression is

IT FUCKING SUCKS.

"Too Late."

It's a deadly combination mixing alcohol with anger
I look myself in the eyes of a mirror and all I see looking back is a stranger
Who are you?
Because you're not the girl I often pretend to be
You are a girl so sad and depressed, you are not a friend to me
You are a bitch,
Cause you manipulate my mind into cutting up my wrists
Into hating who I am, every curve and every inch
Into drinking all my problems till they're gone or that they're fixed
Into seeking validation from a stranger and his dick
You must really hate me...
And I wish I knew what I did
Because even on my enemies I would never wish them this
This, silent cry that breaks every bone in your body down
The feeling of holding it all in so you can let it all out
When you're on the floor of your room, hoping someone hears the music
Or hears the faint screams for help right before you fucking lose it
With the scissors to your wrist ready to abuse it

You hope someone barges in, but they never fucking do it

|

they never fucking do it.

To Everyone I've Ever Loved,

Inhale . . . exhale
Everybody makes it look so simple
It's like I remember to breathe in then get lost
somewhere in the middle
I forget where I am and lose control of my
surroundings
I'm in a pool of my emotions and I can't stop from
drowning
I can't stop and rationalize to find a rhyme or reason
I can't remember the last day I had my time or freedom
I can't remember the last day I took a deep sigh
I can't remember the last day I spent without tears
in my eyes
I don't know what it feels like to be "normal"
To not have to battle between thoughts of suicide
and morals
To not be labeled as too sensitive or overly dramatic
My feelings are what I said, MINE so don't call me
problematic
Until you know what it feels like to be underwater
breathing
Till you know what it feels like to be wide awake and
sleeping
Till you know that breath of relief when you see
yourself and you're bleeding
And you've let out all your tears but your insides
are screaming
For help
Help me . . .

It's been a struggle for quite some time
Having to fight off the demons that consume my mind
They've abused me, they've out done me
They've consumed me, they've become me
I smile so wide to cover up all my scars
And by all means I know that my life isn't hard
But what's hard is this pressure
Of having to have it all together
When you're screaming out for help and all they say
is "feel better"
It's easy to be misunderstood
When outside looking in all you see is the good
You can't see it, or grab it
But I feel it, I have it
I look in the mirror and I don't recognize myself
I have this look of evil that calls for superuser help
And it's scary,
So scary...
To have everyone around you and all you think of
is what they'll say when you're buried
You see nothing but darkness and you're so close
to the end
God wrote out my invite and I'm just waiting
for it to send
Please send
Just take me by car, bus, or plane
I just need to see that "better place" cause
I can't take anymore pain
To everyone I've ever loved, please understand I
feel alone
And nothing will make me happy till I see my name
Carved in stone

AS I lay on my bed, throwing used tissues in the trash
I try to think of things that used to make me laugh
And it's not working
God, why isn't it working
It's not fair to feel the pain of a thousand people hurting
To not tell a soul because you don't want them burdened
I've been so strong before but I am such a weak person
I pretend and joke and kid, like everything's just dandy
Cause my feelings are too raw for anyone to understand me
So I broke ties and burnt bridges
Told lies and made decisions
And I've decided . . .
Today's the day ~~I kill myself~~

I stay alive.

Love always,
    Jess

"It's Never Too Late."

It's hard for her to feel any different
Everyone showers her in compliments, but she doesn't have their vision
She wants to love herself, it's all she ever wishes
But she finds comfort in her pain and every poem she's ever written
She's gifted
It's too bad she can't agree
She beats herself up daily going through all the extremes
And you can tell her that she's worth it, but it's something she won't believe
'Cause it's the most beautiful people who have the lowest self-esteem
And wow, is she beautiful
She's got this burning passion inside her that shines clear right through
her eyes
And this crooked gapped tooth smile that she tries so hard to hide
And this laugh, she's got this laugh that she hates but is so rich in its quality
And she knows she loves herself somewhere deep inside subconsciously
She's just broken from her past, and she's just trying to make it through it
She's fighting to love herself, but depression just beats her to it
She's just looking for a reason not to break one day and lose it
And finally see her beauty the way everyone around her views it
She can do it, she's a fighter
I've seen her fight far worse than this

But to love yourself is a job and I don't think you know how hard it is
It's every day, overtime even when you're tired
The kind of job where you can't quit or ever end up fired
It's demanding, and exhausting being the only one of the sidelines
They say you should love yourself but never gave her any guidelines
SHE IS TRYING...
In the best way she knows how
**It's never too late to love yourself because she is starting to right
now.**

ABOUT
JESSICA M. PAYES

Jessica Payes is a spoken word artist and author, featuring in various open mics and competing in poetry slams around New York City. When not writing or performing, Jessica is a social worker helping families and children navigate life with mental health diagnoses.

In her debut collection, *Manipulated*, Jessica highlights the importance of mental health and its effect in a raw and unfiltered way, being open with her journey of depression hoping readers know they, too, are stronger than their pain.

Jessica is currently working on multiple projects including visual arts, painting, a second poetry collection, and a debut novel.

www.ingramcontent.com/pod-product-compliance
Lightning Source LLC
Chambersburg PA
CBHW020339130626
46549CB00003B/1221